To Andrea
My Dear Friends-
Happy anniversary,
May You Be Always
Blessed With Love,
Joy And Laughter

Emerson Megans

Heart and Soul

To Empower Women
is to Live

A collection of poems
to celebrate women

May they inspire men to
embrace them with desire and
love

Emerson Meyers

Library of Congress Control Number:		2009914304
ISBN:	Hardcover	978-1-4500-0971-3
	Softcover	978-1-4500-0970-6
	Ebook	978-1-4500-0972-0

To order additional copies of this book, contact:
Xlibris Corporation
1-888-795-4274
www.Xlibris.com
Orders@Xlibris.com
71600

Heart and Soul

Designer and
Photographer:
Emerson Meyers

Credits

Dedicated to
"White Angel"

Thanks to the Creator for giving to me
all of my gifts.

Thanks to my Father and Mother
for saying "Yes" to my birth.

Special thanks to Mary, Joan, Nena, Andy
and Kelly for their immeasurable
support on this project. May their
lives be always blessed with peace,
joy, love and harmony.

Many thanks to all those who have
understood my vision and have
acknowledged me on this journey of
enlightenment.

True Love Cannot

Survive Without

Respect

Heart and Soul

is an exquisite gift book
which has been written specifically
for the empowerment of women.

Through these poems and writings, I do hope
that this book may serve two purposes.

First, to let women know that once upon
a time men respected, loved, honored and
adored them without measure. It is simply that too
many men have forgotten this fact, however, all things
that are forgotten can be remembered.

Second, for those men who have lost this
memory, for those who find it difficult
expressing such delicate sensitivities, I do hope that
this book may assist them in acknowledging
and embracing women with desire and love
for the contributions which they continuously
make to our lives.

For those relationships that are already experiencing
Bliss, these poems can add more fuel to the fire.
For those that are broken and dismal, they can mend
them effectively, giving them life, romance, intimacy and
a fulfilling future again. And for those
adolescents that are embarking on new
relationships, this book can really open their
consciousness and shift their experiences to
an altered state of enlightenment.

"To Empower Women Is To Live"

What is life without love
What is love without passion
Without passion we are
Dead inside.

My Poetry

My approach to men and women enjoying happy and everlasting relationships is through love and romantic poetry. It is a universal and very powerful language which is spiritual in nature, and touches the Heart, Soul and Essence of the human being. These poems contain a healing energy which when offered can vitalize relationships. I have been told by many that they have a certain way of reaching deep inside women and men who have read this work.

"Heart and Soul" has been put to the test with my audience and the response has always been overwhelmingly positive, followed by a deep desire to have this little precious gem published. The goal is to assist men and women in relationships to achieve Eternal Bliss.

"The Word Becomes Flesh"

To love is to serve
To serve is to love
To love is everything

Wisdom

If men want to live forever within the hearts of women, even after death, they must possess compassion coupled with the desire to respect, to praise, to honor and above all, to love them without measure. In return women will serve them without end. Living to serve each other is the most essential key to the success of happy, healthy, and fulfilling relationships.

"To Empower Women Is To Live"
"Each Woman Is Unique,
Each Woman Is Beautiful"

The tree of hope
Wears branches of faith
And in time will bear
Love's sweetest fruit
Eternal Bliss

Never Ending Praise

To all the women who have touched
My heart on my journey through this life . . .
"I thank them"

For all the women that have yearned
To be respected, honored and loved . . .
"I bow to them"

To all the women in the universe who
Have allowed me to share these words
Of inspiration with them
"They have honored me"

Contents

Women

Women are God's gift to men, and we that are men too often do not recognize this precious gift. It was very early in the tender years of my youth that this realization became an important part of my life, and today it has brought me to this point of serving and empowering women through my writing. There is not a day that goes by where I do not elevate and honor women in some small way. We need to do this everyday, for not only is it so vital to them, but it is very beneficial to us men. It enriches our lives and fuels our relationships with wonder, happiness and fulfillment. Where there is laughter, it increases the level of joy. Where there is pain, it can remove the darkness and enlighten the heart. Wherever there is love, it feeds the soul and gives our lives more purpose and meaning.

So let us take a short journey together. Let us show our women how much we love, honor, respect, and need them. Let us show them that we would die for them if necessary.

To Empower Women Is To Live

"I do love you so much that there is no more room left in my heart to confess my love for thee." "I promise to continue loving you even after death." "Loving you is like prayer, so sacred, so pure, so divine."

Thy love and mine

Shall binds us

Together . . . forever

Freedom

I do pray for the day
When men can stop and say
"Now . . . I truly understand . . .
For I was once blind,
But today I can see"

All women must be treated
With Respect, Honor, Adoration . . .
And above all . . . Love
May God always bring
Peace and Harmony
To both women and men,
For they belong together
And should not live
Without each other

Ever Devoted

Your Heart is pure
Your Heart is so fine
I do hope your Heart
Will always be mine
I surrender to you
My Dearly Beloved
On my knees I promise
To be ever devoted
And if you shed
A tear from pain
My loving kiss
Will not be in vain
I will caress you tenderly
And fill you with Love
So tenderly
Like soft feathers of a dove
To love you to adore you
Is my one and only Plea
My Heart my Soul
They both belong to thee

Tender Embrace

Your every tender embrace
Feeds my heart with a fire
Each breath that I take
Consumes me with desire
I do live for your love
Sweet passion from above
Let me melt in your arms
You thrill me with your charms
So carve your name into my heart
Promise me dear
We will never ever part
Do caress me dear caress me
My bosom's hungry to please thee
Warm breath on my lips
Soft hands on my hips
I worship you my Goddess
You bring me such Bliss

Strength

So great is your wisdom
Your whole life's a sacrifice
I feel your heart bleeding
I see the tears in your eyes
Yet your love still remains
Yet your strength never fades
Your forgiveness lingers on
Your shoulders are so strong
Your smile is so warm
Your touch soft like a love song
What can I give to thee
To free the pain that I see
How can I serve thee
Shall I slay a lion
Shall I cross a stormy sea
Tell me please tell me
I would lay down my life for thee
So willingly upon
Bended knee

Bride

My dear sweet
Darling
Let me lay down by
Your side
My Honey
My Heaven
My Life
My sweet Darling
Bride

Endless Desire

I come bearing a gift to please thee so anxiously
With love's hunger and thirst so willingly unselfishly
My heart it is pounding, my breath is on fire
Would you accept it, embrace it with endless desire
I promise to take thee on a journey of pleasure
Your body I worship, I adore, I do treasure
Your soft skin so warm, so sweet, so heavenly
Each day I pray that your heart will love me
I long to taste your lips upon me
Your every pleasure remains my solemn duty
Gracefully we soar to heaven affectionately
My endless desire for you is so preciously divine
Halleluiah, Halleluiah God's love doth shine

White Swan

My beautiful White Swan
 So full of such grace
There is no one in heaven
 That can ever take your place
Your skin is like silk
 Your lips sweet as honey
My arms are awaiting
 They were meant for you only

Free

I long and wish to see the day
    When you can feel so free to say
I do love you and live
    I do want you and give
To me your soul, your heart
    For at that very moment we will truly start
A life full of magic, a life full of wonder
    And night after night we will lay in bed and
Ponder
    Of every desire to keep this all consuming fire
Growing and burning now and forever
    Beneath the moon and starry sky
I will love you my dear, until the day I die

I was once dead
Now I am alive
For your love has
Made me whole

I will read precious poetry
To you at night
I will confess my love for
You with delight

My heart bleeds for you
My spirit grieves for you
Whenever you are gone
Come home to me
My precious Queen

With joy and all humility
I pledge to thee
This band of gold
Please trust in me . . .

I love you I want you
For heaven's sake
I would die for you

Come sit with me close
By the fire
Let me touch you, hold you
Feel my desire

I will tenderly kiss
Your crimson lips . . .
And melt into the midst
Of Bliss

Let us enjoy the happiness
Of discovering love
Together

My love, you give me
Hope when there is none
Beside me you guide me
All my battles
They are won

I am fulfilled when you
Are happy my love
For never have I ever loved
Another as pure, as true

Give me your hand,
Your pain, your sorrow
I promise to love thee
Way past tomorrow

Ever lasting devotion I
Pledge to thee
With my heart and soul
I do cherish thee

Save My Soul

I need someone
To save my soul
I need someone to
Have and to hold
Bitter sweet is my troubled
Heart Beat
How long must I wait
To be ever complete

I have sailed vast oceans
I have crossed stormy seas
Is there truly someone out there
I am so willing to please
So many sleepless hours
I just toss and I turn
Too many endless nights of being alone
So I beg you Dear Spirits
My arms are open wide
I implore you Dear Spirits
Please be my guide

For my heart's been ready for
A very long time
Please end this grave pain
Please send me Someone
To be Mine

A gentle knock on my door
I run with much haste
And there stood an Angel
So full of such Grace
I bow before her
Then took her fair hand
I embraced her tenderly
Then gave her a
Wedding Band
Dear heavenly Angel
You have saved my soul
Dear heavenly Angel
I am yours to behold

Spell

Why does my heart beat
That oh so strange beat
I melt, I weep, let me lay
My head at your feet
Your breath makes me
Quiver
Your touch makes me
Shiver
I can never say never
Am I under your spell
Forever

Angels Sing

Rejoice my love our time has come
Heavens' Angels sing
Divine church bells ring
And at the Altar we do pledge
Our vows
To love, to cherish, to adore, to endow
My hands they clasp
Your hands in time
Our lives forever will always
Intertwine
I love you now
I loved you then
I pray to God this Bliss never ends
For you are my darling
My one true love
You are my Everything
A gift from above
Halleluiah, Halleluiah
Divine church bells still ring
Halleluiah, Halleluiah
Heavens' Angels still sing

And When I Die

And when I die
Please tell the world
That when I loved
I did love
With sincerity
For there was no more
Room left
In my heart to Confess
My love for Thee

My Love

My love
It carries a sword of it's own
It begs for connection
Then time to be alone
Time to worship you
It won't be in vain
Time to adore you
It will take away your pain
It floods you with it's kind embrace
It promises to take you
To a heavenly place
It's fragile and strong
Please stretch out your hand
Touch me so gently
Like the sea and the sand
You have felt my lips on your bosom
So sweet
Come lay down beside me
Let's be complete

Queen

Come to me my beautiful
    Queen of Queens
In pomp and glory
    Even the Gods have never seen
I will kindle a fire
    Make me burn with desire
We will laugh, we will sing
    We will love, we will play
Forever more my darling
    Our love hath no decay

No . . . Never Dear

When you close your eyes
    Do you see my face
When you lie in bed
    Am I in your space
Let me breathe your air
    Let me stroke your hair
Can I be your fantasy
    It could be a reality
And when I die
    Will my love die too
No . . . No never dear
    For it will always
Belong to only you

Glorious Star

My thankful heart
Is beating fast
My joyful mind
Desires you lass
My aching body
Awaits you patiently
My arms are longing
To hold you so gently
The days and nights linger on and on
Your voice I remember
Is like a heavenly song
You bow to me in all humility
I worship your divinity
Your majesty unselfishly
A glorious star has led you to me
My breath I beg you
Please take it freely
I praise you my beloved
Let me kneel down before thee
My flesh it is dying
For your warm touch so anxiously
My honey my bride
I want to be yours
Completely

May I live forever loving you
For love has never been
More delicious . . .

Loving you is such
Sweet surrender
Your faith in me I will
Always treasure

Please stain my heart
With your loving kiss
Your kiss, your kiss, I
Cannot resist

Blame me not for loving
You dear
I want to keep you
Ever so near

I do truly love you
I do honestly adore you
I promise to love you
Until eternity

My love will flood you
With it's kind embrace
It promises to take you
To a heavenly place

Please hold on and
Don't let go
My strength is more than
You will ever know

I will dress you in silk
There is no measure
Your soft skin my love
It brings me such pleasure

I promise to love you
Even after death
My darling

My love for you has
No beginning it has no end
All my life with you
I want to spend

Night after night
I lay and ponder
Our heavenly ride is
Full of such wonder

Hold me, kiss me
Love me, want me
I need to be consumed by thee

My Yearning

The night gets so cold
When you are not near to hold
Time lingers on
So long when you are gone
The world stops turning
Can you take away this burning
My heart it is breaking
Do you not see my arms are yearning
Always clinging to the last memory
Can you get inside of me
I worship you my dear Princess
My lips long for your kisses
The wings of true love
The spirit of a dove
The pain wounds me like Spears
My flesh my blood
A river of Tears

To Serve You Only

As I lay in my solitude just thinking of
Thee
My heart peers through crystal panes
As I joyously see
Thy tender eyes looking gently back
At me
Beloved my beloved do look inside
Your heart
I willingly stand there trembling
Struck by Cupid's dart
Your love has captured the melody that
Moves me
Now I shall live
To love To serve You only

Angel, Angel

Angel, Angel keep me safe
    Angel, Angel please make haste
Angel, Angel would you shed a tear for me
    Angel, Angel will you always be a guide to me
I awake at night and feel you near
    Protecting me with your wings, I do know you
Care
    And when I am lost, will you help me find my
Way
    Back to your arms, where I will always want to
Stay
    Forever, I promise to be true to thee
My spirit feels free when you are near to me
    Your love gives me strength
Your love keeps me sane
    Your love heals my wounds when ever there is
Pain
    So Angel, Angel when the day is done
When my joys, my sorrows have all been spun
    I look upon your smiling face
I invite you to enter my humble space
    For there is no one more that I adore
Angel, Dear Angel, I will continue to love you
    More and more

All Consumed

Oh constant heart, please be true to me
May this day never leave my memory
I am all consumed by a love so, so rare
Day dreaming in time, I don't have a care

The shadows of night just go on forever
I anxiously await my love's next encounter
My blood is raging there's a poison in my veins
How can I stop this madness I am going
Insane

I long for your touch, I long for your kiss
Your beauty is so overwhelming I cannot resist
Take all of my soul Take every part
I surrender to you dear I give you my heart

Upon Bended Knee

May our wedding night be full of bliss
   All our dreams, all our desires, sealed with a
Loving kiss
   May our beating hearts soar beyond heaven's gate
Our hungry bodies climbing to an altered State
   May God be always present at this blessed union
And every day of our lives be free of confusion
   Happy is the day when we can run wild and free
Happy was the day I pledged my love to thee
   So willingly, upon bended knee

Desire

This night is so haunting
Memories of love are
So taunting
I lay in my bed
Can't get you out of my head
The wings of temptation
Stimulate my sensation
Keep me wanting for more
Burning desire
Please quench my fire
It is you I adore

Precious Gift

Dear sweet little angel
How can the world not see
You have been such a blessing
A precious gift from heaven to me
Your eyes sparkle like moon beams
Your innocent laughter
Touches all dreams
You warm my heart
Your gentle smile is so fair
Always will I cherish you
Always will I keep you
I love you my dear

Day after day
I do earnestly pray
Forever more my darling
Our love hath no decay

May our beating hearts
Soar beyond heaven's gate
Our hungry bodies climb
To an altered state

Our wedding night will be
Full of such bliss
Our dreams, our desires
Sealed with a loving kiss

Let me kiss your hand
Let me kiss your feet
Let me lay my head on
Your bosom so sweet

I will shelter you from
Life's thunderstorms
My shoulders are strong
In my arms you belong

My sweet darling . . . .
I do love you more
Than life itself

Your love leaves me
Breathlessly, endlessly
Longing for more

I do love you now
I have loved you then
I pray to God that our
Love never ends

Do carve your name
Into my heart
Promise me dear that
We will never ever part

Our hearts our souls
May they bond together
And Heavens' Angels celebrate
Our blessed union forever

Where does this passion
End within me
How can I now my love
Deny

Your beauty transcends
All space and time
Your spirit speaks of heaven
And all that is divine

For Heaven's Sake

There is a thunder pounding
In my heart
My head is spinning
I don't know where to Start
I love you I adore you
For heaven's sake
I would die for you

A fire's raging through my veins
The emptiness dear God
I can't stand the pain
I wait and I wait
What is to be my plight
Please deliver me dear
From this cold dark night

I toss and I turn
I just can't find sleep
To live and die
My soul to weep

Heart of My Heart

Though tears of joy may run
Down my cheek
Let me cradle your hand
Your soft bosom leaves
Me weak
And when I rest my weary head
As I lay across my empty bed
That certain part of me goes dead
I feel a hole inside my soul
And I wish you were near
To have and to hold
Please shackle my heart
To your heart
I surrender to you my dear
I surrender each part
Of me can't you see
I live and die then live again
For your love sets me free

Oh God Please

Your smile is worth a thousand kisses
Your eyes speak of such tender graces
So soft is your touch your lips so divine
How sacred is your heart
I wish it were mine
I search deep within my soul
To find the truth
I just can't pretend
I am in love with you
Your innocence so pure
All time does stand still
I am falling apart against my own will
Of course I do know you belong to another
It is fate that's created
This awesome encounter
I get down on my knees and pray
Oh God please
Send me someone like thee to love to serve
My heart longs to be free

Today I Found My One True Love

From where you came I do know not
    My heart's inflamed, you have filled that Empty spot
    Your soft sweet voice, your tranquil smile
I do feel your spirit, please, would you stay a while
    I dream precious dreams of you at night
My mind's enveloped with sheer delight

    A rose I picked for you today
What joy, what beauty, I felt it say
    "This is the essence of the love I am desiring"
Untolding, unfolding, awaiting for embracing
    As I stroked it's petals so delicate, so rare
My bosom went full, my breath, I declare
    Ran racing upward to heaven in fear

Your ring of gold forever, I cherish divine
    May God permit . . . My love to be yours . . .
Your love to be mine . . .
    For I promise to give thee my heart, my
Soul
    Will you take it and keep it
It is yours to behold
    Today I found my one true love
Thank you dear God for your gift from above

Breathlessly

I dream a dream of you at night
Beneath starry sky and pale
Moon light
Often have I wondered through
The Portals of your heart
Caressing white doves as I gaze
Through each part
How Heavenly what Divinity
I search helplessly
For your love leaves me
Breathlessly
Endlessly longing for embracing
So affectionately
I confess my love
I am yours completely

Beloved Spirit

Beloved spirit
I am calling out
Your name
How could I be so blind
How could I be so vain
I am so sorry
If I have offended thee
You know you mean
The world to me
I do trust you dear
With my arms open wide
All my life I want to be
Right by your side
I do love you now
I have loved you then
I pray to God
That our love never ends

Hugs and Kisses

Warm hugs and long kisses
    Tight embraces, sweet reminisces
Hot bodies intertwine
    Hearts full of divine
Take hold of my hand
    Let's write love notes in the sand
All our vows are renewed
    All our dreams do come true
When ever we say . . . "I do"

My Beautiful Queen
How could my life be the same
You are warm like my blood
You run through my veins

Dear God . . . May this precious love
Bind us together forever

I feel your presence
With every step that I make
Your essence I taste with every
Breath that I take

Warm breath on my lips
Soft hands on my hips
I adore you my Goddess, you
Bring me such bliss

One hour of your love is
Such great content
I am convinced my dear
That you were heaven sent

I am sorry my darling
But I was wrong
Please forgive me for I
Do know where I belong

Loving you is like prayer
So sacred, so sincere
So divine

When I am in your arms
The world stops turning
Please Quench my thirst
Satisfy my yearning

Our heated passion
Burning bright
Endlessly growing
Into the night

A glorious star has
Led you to me
My breath I beg you
Please take it freely

Your love gives me strength
Your love keeps me sane
Your love always takes
Away my pain

My honey, my bride
Come lay down
By my side
My love I simply
Cannot hide

Beautiful Swan

As I left the garden so fair and green
My bleeding heart was cleft in twain
Your silent spirit touched
My soul so deeply
My will it questioned should I stay
Or should I go respectfully
So beautiful a swan of bronze that you are
Soft skin of gold I can taste from afar
Your lips of lush your voice is so kind
Bathe me with your kisses
Your mouth's so divine
I have loved you once upon a time
In a dream
You spun your magic
I surrendered to your scheme
I melt before thee there is no measure
Your Life, Your Soul
They are both such a treasure

Yes you are a very precious treasure indeed
If heaven permits, you are the cure
For my need
Your dear tender feet so delicate, so rare
Can I kiss them, can I caress them
I will always love you I declare
So now Beautiful Swan
You know what's in my heart
How can my life be the same
These feelings won't ever depart
I have loved you once upon a time
In a dream
I promise to love thee
To adore thee
My precious beautiful Queen

Amanda Angelica

Your soft eyes speak of Heaven
Your spirit touches the heart
Your undying faith has no boundaries
Your light beams it streams
Please never depart
How angelic is your voice
It speaks such compassion
Your precious innocence
Is pure and void of expectation
Your silent smile
So tender so charming so inviting
All melodies come alive
With your gentle embracing
Dear Fair Maiden
The world has been awaiting your coming
Deny it not your wisdom
Your love and your caring
For you give us all hope
In this time of sorrow
Your presence your reverence
Make us thank God
For tomorrow

Because

It's all because of you, you see
It's all because of you and me
And all the love I do have for thee
With this love of ours, we will
Always be free
For I believe we were truly
Truly Meant to be

So Glad You Are Mine

And when you ask me if I do love thee
    I simply would say from the very first day
When you stood by the bay
    My lonesome heart sought after your heart
With hope and with fear
    Wishing you will always be near
We walked hand in hand counting shells
    In the sand, your eyes were as warm as the sun
On my cheek, so often did I gaze into them and
    Could hardly speak
Your beauty, so pure, your poise so divine
    Always gently my love, I am so glad you are
        Mine

My Love is Thine

Heart of my heart
It's my true love's birthday
Let us gather up rose buds
Let us romp and play
Have I told you lately
How much I love thee
Our destinies are linked
So faithfully don't you see
In lush meadows of green
We will frolic and dine
I do pledge to thee my love
It will always be thine

Beautiful Bronze Goddess

How many times have I gazed into your eyes
    And found myself so lost inside
So long have I lingered at your sensuous bosom
    Tasting it's skin, I cannot hide
I love you I want you
    For God's sake I would die for you
I have tried many times
    To get you out of my mind
Still you keep returning
    Leaving me helplessly yearning
You are so divine,
    Help me please help me
Be free of this pain that I feel
    I need to wrap my loving arms around thee
To reveal this love that's so real
    Dear Beautiful Bronze Goddess
Do look into my eyes
    Can you see my heart bleeding
What is to be my demise
    Our spirits will fly so high past the sky
In your arms so truly I do want to die
    So please don't deny me please satisfy me
There is a fire that is burning
    It is raging within me
I promise to adore thee, to serve thee
    Let us set our love free

My Love, My Wife, My Life

Thou art so precious indeed to me
  How did I live so long without thee
Now that I have found you
  I promise my love will always be true
You are my love, my wife, my life
  I pray to God we live without strife
How did I live so long without thee
  Our hearts, our souls, such sweet destiny
I want to vanish within your kiss
  Your tender embrace I cannot resist
For you are my love, you are my life
  Thank you dear God for my darling wife

Emma Angelica Precious Gem

A Precious Gem
You are to me
I wish there were a way
The world could see
Your Angelic eyes
Looking gently back at me
Thank you
For your dear sweet love
Thank you for that beautiful
White Dove
For I have been waiting
A long time for thee
You will always remain
A Precious Gem
To me

My Darling Bride

My beautiful Lady, my Angel, my Darling Bride
I do come before thee upon bended knee
To confess my undying love for thee
You are my one and only true love
You are the reason that I live
For your love gives me strength
To fight my daily battles
Your love keeps me sane
It takes away all pain
So please take my love for I do give it freely
I do want to spend the rest of my life
Loving thee, honoring thee, adoring thee
I want to call out your name
Always with desire
For my heart and soul they both belong to thee

As we clasp our hands in time at this altar
May God bless this sacred union and be
Always present to guide us
Through our lives together
You are very precious to me
My darling, my Maiden
And I always want you to be at my side
To care for you, to support you through
Your trials and your desires
May you love me without measure
For my love belongs to you and you alone
I do love you my Angel
My Soul Mate, my Darling Bride

To Serve Is Not To Be A Slave

Can men serve women and still remain masculine? Yes indeed, that is an absolute fact. No man has ever lost their masculinity in the service of women. The truth is that men show more strength and compassion within themselves when women are served by them. Men can be strong and yet be gentle. Men can have firm convictions and still be compassionate. Men can demonstrate assertiveness and still be kind and charitable. Men can exercise determination and dedication and still possess the desire to embrace women with love and affection.

Since the beginning of time, women have been taught to serve, they have been expected to serve, they have been forced to serve men. It is now time that men learn to serve women with desire and love. If men would seek deep inside their hearts and souls they would truly see that honestly the time has come for the scales of balance to change, to shift and become equal through serving women. We can be in the service of another and not be a slave to that person because slavery is forced servitude.

To offer to serve is beautiful and shows strength, charity, love and compassion. It makes us bigger and better human beings, especially when the one we are serving responds with gratitude and love. We can serve each other and still remain whole and unfragmented. So I repeat, slavery is forced servitude, to willingly offer to serve is to love and is totally opposite.

"We Need To Serve One Another"

What is life
Without love . . .
Emptiness . . . Really . . .

Thank you dear God
for your gifts
from above.

Get Published, Inc!
Thorofare, NJ 08086
12 March, 2010
BA2010071